ARE YOU LOOKING FOR ME?

Spot Nature Naturally

Text and photos by
CHARLENE LEWIS

Photography

Naturally

Supported by the R.E. Sanders SB Fund

GlenMargaret
PUBLISHING

D1511274

Are you looking for me?
I might be hard to see.
Are you looking for me?
I could be on a branch in a tree.
Look at the picture.
Look all around.
I might be sitting on a plant
or next to a rock on the ground.

Do you want to be able to spot animals when you go outside?
Let's get ready now! Let's find out how!

Animals come in all shapes, sizes and colours.
There are **mammals** and **birds** and **reptiles** and **amphibians** and **fish**.
Did you know that insects and spiders are animals too?
They are in the largest group, called **invertebrates**.

When you spot an animal, the colour of its page will tell you
what group it belongs to.

LET'S START SPOTTING!
HERE'S HOW …

Look at this picture first
and see if you can spot me.

When you do,
let's turn the page.
You'll see me up close
and I'll introduce myself.

Here I am!

I am a sparrow. You can spot me in bogs, marshes and farm fields. My nest is usually under roofs or in the hollows of trees. I eat yummy things like snails, moths and worms.

Good spotting!

Let's go find some more....

ARE YOU LOOKING FOR US?

Here we are!

We're white-tailed deer. We're called that because the underside of our tail is white and you can see it when we leap and run. That's called **flagging** — it's our way to signal an alarm to other deer and help fawns to follow their mothers.

Here I am!

Hi, I'm a white admiral butterfly. You can spot me in places like parks and gardens — wherever there are sweet-smelling flowers. I like to taste them with my feet. How do you taste things?

ARE YOU LOOKING FOR ME?

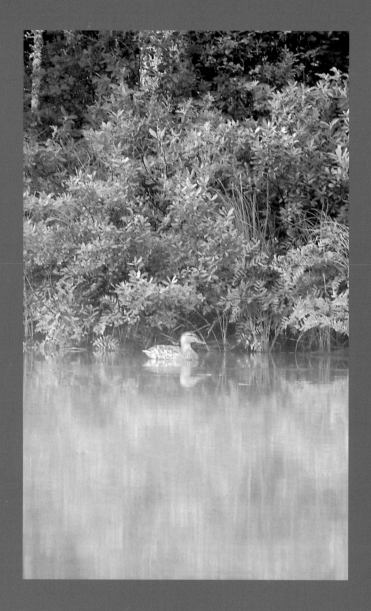

Quack, quack. Yes, I'm a duck. I'm a female mallard. You can find me on water, like a lake or a river. You might even spot me flying in the air but when I first started out, I was an egg in a nest. Can you quack like I do?

Here I am!

I'm a pickerel frog, not a toad. Do you know how to tell the difference? I'm narrower and smoother than a toad and my eyes bulge. You can find me in and around water. My feet are webbed. Are your feet webbed too?

ARE YOU LOOKING FOR ME?

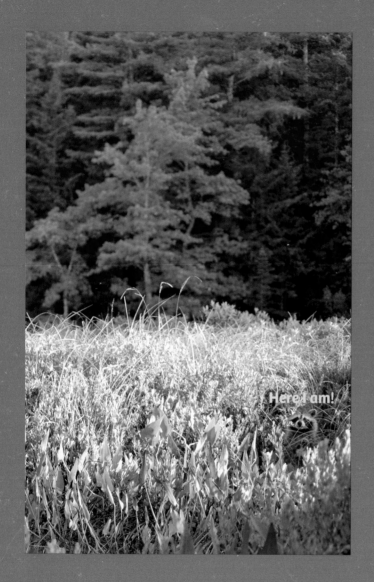

Here I am!

I look like I'm wearing a mask! I'm a raccoon. You can spot me in swamps, forests, and even in the city, but you'd have to be up late because I'm nocturnal. That means that I prefer to move around at night. I have long claws and a bushy, ringed tail.

ARE YOU LOOKING FOR ME?

Here I am!

Have you seen me jump? I'm a grasshopper. You can spot me in fields and meadows — wherever I can find some vegetation to eat. I can make songs by rubbing my wings or legs together. I have five eyes, so I can see in all directions.

We are pileated woodpeckers. There are two of us in that old tree. You might hear us before you see us because we make loud pecking sounds with our beaks when we search for ants to eat. Can you make a pecking sound?

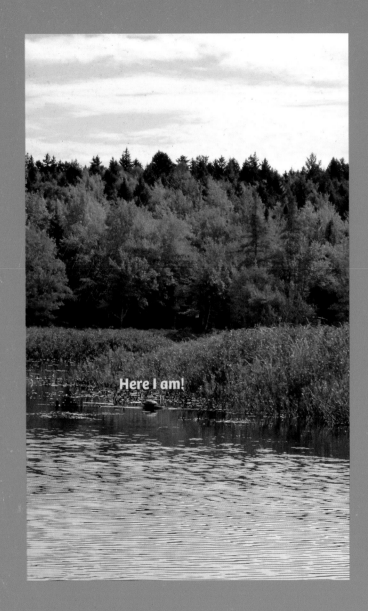

Here I am!

I'm a painted turtle. I'm part of the reptile family, which means that I'm cold-blooded, and need to warm up in the sun. You might find me sunning myself on a big rock or log, like I am doing here. How do you get warmed up?

I'm a goldenrod crab spider. I'm not an insect. I eat insects for food. I catch them in the webs that I weave. I have two more legs than an insect, which means that I have...eight legs! How many legs do you have?

What did you spot first, the red squirrel or the bird, which is called a flycatcher? They both showed up at the lake to get some water to drink. Where do you get your drinking water?

ARE YOU LOOKING FOR ME?

Here I am!

I'm the insect called a darner dragonfly, but I'm not a flying dragon. With my bulging eyes I can see really well. I need to see what's moving so that I don't collide with anything when I'm flying.

Here I am!

I'm a rabbit though some people also call us bunnies. We like eating grass and wild flowers. Most of us like to hop around at dawn and dusk. That's when you are more likely to see us. Do you hop too?

Here I am!

Whooo, whooo! I'm a barred owl. I'm nocturnal, just like the raccoon, so I'm pretty hard to find. When I fly I am a lot quieter than most other birds. You can spot me in trees where I call out a sound called a hoot. Can you hoot too?

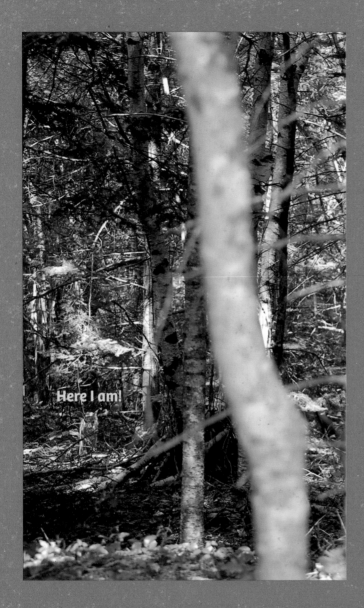

Here I am!

I'm a fawn, a baby deer. You can spot me in the forest or meadows where my mom gets me to stay until she comes back. If you come too close I might run away and then she can't find me. Thanks for just looking.